Francesca Woodman

Endpapers: **Study for Space^2**, Providence, Rhode Island, 1975-1978, detail

Francesca WOODMAN

Fondation Cartier pour l'art contemporain   **SCALO** Zurich—Berlin—New York

Contents

Original contact sheet, Italy, 1977-1978, detail

Rome, Italy, 1977-1978

Preface   The work of Francesca Woodman is as dazzling and as magical as an apparition. It is fascinating; it compels us with its clarity, with the trenchant precision of its presence. There is none of the affectedness that we might expect of an artist who spent so much time photographing her own body. Executed from when she was 13 to the time of her suicide at the age of 22 (1972-1981), her work expresses itself through the landscapes of places as different as Rome and New York, Providence and MacDowell Colony.

Displaying to view the ghostly and evanescent presence of her own body in movement, Francesca Woodman suggests the passing and the ephemeral, the transitory and fragile. Rather than capturing a suspended moment, these photographs allow us to see time in all its elusiveness. The way she frames her shots fragments and isolates her subjects and show the urgency of representation. Always wanting to disappear, Francesca Woodman melts into and loses herself in her surroundings, or, in other places, plays with the idea of mutilation and hints at the violent serenity of a fragmented body.

In this exhibition, the most comprehensive to date, the Fondation Cartier pour l'art contemporain presents some hundred photographs, as well as about ten large-scale works on blue or sepia paper, and the original design for her book *Some Disordered Interior Geometries* which was published in 1981. Her brief but accomplished work can thus be seen here displaying all its power.

This exhibition could not have happened without the work, devotion and complicity of Betty and George Woodman; may they accept this as a sign of our sincere gratitude. Our thanks go also to the authors of the catalog, Philippe Sollers, David Levi Strauss, Elizabeth Janus and Sloan Rankin, as well as all the others who made this work possible.

Hervé Chandès
Curator of the Fondation Cartier pour l'art contemporain

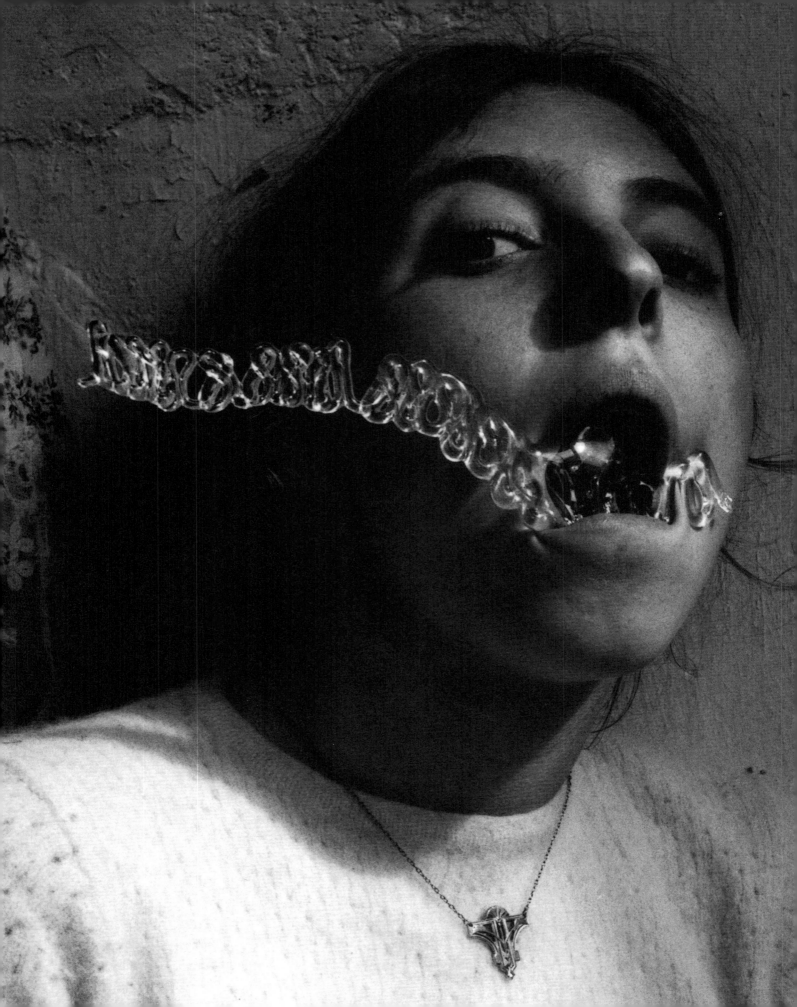

The Sorceress
Philippe Sollers

From the very beginning, Francesca Woodman places herself in

the strange world of an anti-picture. She emerges from obscurity, crosses through the mirror and materialises for a moment in a world twisted with anxiety. She treats herself like an apparition. In this space that we others accept as reality, she shines more brightly than we, surrounded by mere cameo figures and shadows. What choice has she but to photograph the event that brings her forth? For it cannot be told in any other way. A verbal narrative would be too complicated, too slow, incomprehensible; it would not demonstrate to what extent the image wrought from a false reality is superior, why and how our lives are a charade that is conformist and banal. A special *mise-en-scène* is required to destabilise this pantomime, to return it to its innocence, its primordiality, its explosive humour. She is bold, Woodman; she is more naked than anyone else. She has decided to disturb this sleep walk that is life.

Just look at how she *introduces* herself: naked and on her knees, in Rome, at the corner of a wall, very slightly turned towards a white flower that stands upright. Not an ordinary lily but an *arum* lily. You already know how suggestive this flower is, I don't need to draw a picture. It looks as if an angel had surreptitiously deposited the symbol and left without saying a word; but it was Woodman, of course, who had given this baroque present to herself. She is not really waiting, for nothing will come to pass: she is at this moment an inaccessible virgin. In this photograph she shows how much she has learned from the many artists of the eternal city, Bernini among them, who tried to represent women's private parts. Another photograph shows her pressing herself against a wall, a maleficent silhouette that looks like something out of Uccello's *Legend of the Desecration of the Host,* her face covered with a white circle, the floor ritually chequered, while a tortoise crawls forward in a corner. Then we see two girls waiting: it is unclear where they are, but they've just been arrested for a crime or misdemeanour and will face a sentence—the gloves tell the whole story. In another image Francesca is hanging up her photographs in an avant-garde gallery which was not called *Maldoror* for nothing. She seems to belong to the 12th century: she's resolute, completely in control of her steps and her acts of exorcism. What is this next woman doing in a bathtub? We only see her blond hair: the picture is showing us an open coffin. "I show you what you do not see—the body's inner force," says Woodman. "You cannot see me from where I look at myself." So we see her at every age simultaneously: infant, girl, woman and old maid, old woman and then infant again. Contrary to the mass delusion and its levelling propaganda, woman has no real existence—and don't go thinking that's an enviable situation to be in. Sorceress or woman possessed? One has to be able to deal with that urge to take possession. Otherwise it's back into the kitchen—and she's not cut out for that.

When one doesn't exist, except in the impossibility of being an angel (of good or evil, it doesn't really matter), one has a tendency to float, to levitate, for space and weight obey new laws. Woodman is a provocative angel, of course, but she is ironic, not threatening (in fact she will destroy only herself). She does not pronounce profound truths, screams no curses, does not play the oracle or sibyl. There is no ostentation or megalomania, no religiosity, no display of mimed pain or suffering.

Her role is not to intimidate us by crying that there is nothing more than madness, passion, death and horror—that would be vulgar. In other words, there is no guilt (this isn't a Duras novel). She remains constantly dynamic and buoyant. She periodically conceals herself, doesn't take her ordeal seriously, even if (what a terrible image this is) she can represent herself with open mouth, emitting a stream of what look like bubbles. The tomb seems to present no obstacle to her—we see her ghostly form passing straight through it—nor do the bounds of the explicable. She and another woman are shown, for no apparent reason, standing with their dresses open, showing their breasts. She focuses in on a leg on an armchair, but as you look longer at this picture, the armchair seems to disappear. Reality is made to be broken up and to disappear, and it is precisely *this* that has to be photographed when one is absorbed and inspired by the negative. Is the sorceress a saint? Yes—but these days saints and martyrs contrive their own tortures. There is no head above that female torso pinched, as if in some sado-masochistic game, by seven clothes pegs. Woodman experiences flesh precisely. She is not suffering from any kind of hysterical numbness, but obstinately confronts the physical. Someone who knew her describes her thus, "She was an extremely sensual person, very Bataille, very Artaud, very strong, a very physical thing." It's easy to believe. No pity is shown towards anything that is deformed, monstrous or sick (unlike Diane Arbus). She is harsh, but elegant; cruel but without taking it too far. It suddenly occurs to me that I could very well have met her in Rome or New York at the end of the 70s, during her great period of creativity. But it is of no importance: to each his own magic, and mine is blue and white—Chinese—a blue towards which, in fact, she was evolving towards the end.

We should recall those little-understood lines that Rimbaud wrote in the so-called *Lettre du voyant* (1871): "When the infinite servitude of woman is broken, when she lives by and for herself, when man has finally let her go (till now he has been abominable)—then she too will be a poet. Woman launch out into the unknown! Will her worlds of ideas differ from ours? She will find things that are strange, unfathomable, repulsive, delicate; we will take them and understand them."
The time has indeed come to *understand*.

Let us take two examples, almost at random, from a contemporary novel:
"The staircase unravelled under my feet without my reaching any floors. It seemed that I had already been going up for a long time, but at the same time that I was simply not advancing, or even that I was descending into the cellars—where perhaps something even more disconcerting awaited me. I stopped for a second, out of breath. The vertical lines of the stairwell, entangled with the spiralling ribbon of the banister, seemed to arch. The walls curved in new places, as if the straight shaft of the spiral staircase itself followed the rising and falling loops of a grander spiral. The staircase seemed to be all coiled up in a helix-shaped stairwell, even if I wasn't able to completely assure myself of this. The staircase that I was climbing *seemed* to proceed regularly enough, but the great spiral which enclosed it must rise and fall in circular coils, without it being possible for me to know where I was going—this second spiral being perhaps held within the coils of a third great spiral, and so on and so on, up to who knows what level or depth, and in what direction." [1]

Or again:

"The bed came up so close to the window I thought it would break through the glass and carry me away, sheets flapping in the wind, me hanging on to the pillow for dear life. The main roads merged right into the black sky, strings of street lights hung outside my illuminated windows, monuments were silhouetted in relief against the horizon. I felt the pressure of the air against my pillow, churning beneath the bed, and if I spread out my arms, I would float on the breezes, I would let the rising currents carry me with them, I would sense, from the slightest stirrings, the risings of the warm air and the sinkings of the cold. And racing in the hollows of my hands, under my arms, beneath my stomach, holding up my toes, tearing between my fingers, I would feel the slipstream of my flight. Finally, limpid, the sea." [2]

That's the risk. On 19th January 1981, on the threshold of that great cultural decline, the rejection of modernity, Francesca Woodman threw herself from the window of her loft in the East Village. She was twenty-two.

The sorceress works hard. As a photographer she follows Steichen, Stieglitz and Kertész, who opened the way for this composition of instantaneous, fantastic novels. Hell has its own brand of gaiety, its own sort of circus humour. In the novel which I've just quoted, notice the vertigo of all those spirals and the violence of the passage towards window and sea. In a man's writing, one would immediately think this was a narcotic experience. But it's a *normal* woman who writes these lines. Hallucinogenic substances are not required; for space itself is dynamic, and needs no encouragement to fall upon itself, swell up, writhe around and become incensed. Look now at the photographs of the "mad" house of Woodman in Providence (Providence!). A dilapidated fireplace, walls which cry out, and a woman on her knees with her hands against a wall, seen from the back, and commenting, "Then at one point I did not need to translate the notes; they went directly to my hands." The mouth which looks as if it is emitting a saliva-like cord is entitled *Self portrait talking to vince* (how many times did she have to try to get that fabulous shot?). A distorted angel, as we find in Tintoretto, is not an easy thing to photograph, and yet Woodman, like an oak tree in a storm, does it.

That reminds me of a hot summer night in New York during those years. I was on the twelfth floor with a young film actress, brunette and extremely attractive. The window was open, we'd smoked quite a lot of hash, we started to kiss — and she suddenly said to me, her eyes burning and empty, "Throw yourself out and see if it makes me come." It wasn't aggressive, it was more tender. To her disappointment, I led her back inside. She must have realised that I wasn't attracted to her. Of course we didn't see each other again. Such events are both serious and trivial, except when they become tragic, which can happen from time to time. Some of my friends "gave" themselves in such a way. Wrongly, it seems to me, since there is no reason to take such a dive in the name of a problematic female orgasm. Why imagine you need to be, so to speak, the plunging burden of love, or the one who comes to interrupt a bloodlust for the infinite? It's better just to laugh.

And Woodman laughs. The masterpieces of her work are probably the pieces she composed with the model Charlie. Charlie, as in Chaplin. He's a big, easy-going guy whom she makes assume exhibitionist poses in front of mirrors. Francesca likes to have fun. She is taming a big bear. But these photographs are also extremely bold. At the time when she was appropriating this male body for herself and transforming it into a fairground attraction, she was 18 years old. She puts herself into the photograph with him, naked. She is also thinking of Francis Bacon, it's clear, with her boxed and compressed bodies, fish-eye lens distortions and cuboid rooms. What amazing sessions those were with Charlie. One wonders exactly how they got along, this pot-bellied man with his slightly idiotic grin and this adolescent angel, this angelette. Anyway, the evidence is there for us to see. He raises his leg, lies down under a pane of glass, holds a cylindrical object, and, all pleased with himself (that's his job) takes up his pose in front of this madwoman who wants to photograph him (or does she want more?). The mirrors and windows cannot believe their own surfaces—the scene is beautiful, mad, festive, joyful. In a more velvety image of caressing shadows, Woodman represents herself as a traditional "woman-to-be-looked-at," gazing at herself in front of a mirror. We know that men love the shimmer of images. "You'll get all excited about an image, my friend, but you'll never know what lies behind—nothing at all." I like the fact that Francesca was an admiring reader of Proust, as well as a pianist ("I've been playing the piano for a long time, especially variations—Scarlatti, etc.") Her statements are sometimes remarkable for their perspicacity: "I'm interested in the relationships that people have with space." There is a hint of Dreyer, of *Nadja*. You imagine that she studied Charcot's book, *Les Démoniaques dans l'art*. No religiosity, I said: "My only religion is spaghetti." And again, as we hear from someone who knew her, "She wasn't a feminist. She loved men passionately."

I don't like Francesca Woodman, I admire her. She bears witness to a time where experience and the stakes of the game were intense, dangerous, intoxicating. What is there today? AIDS, unemployment, Monica Lewinsky, Hillary, the Oscars, the Palme d'Or, single mothers… The financial markets impose the picture and forbid the anti-picture, the voice of liberty. The Devil has become pathetic and God isn't even here to help him anymore. Farewell, refined sorceress! We will see your work again one day, in another cycle of history. After the "Asian crisis", for example. When the witches' Sabbaths are heard again in the depths of the forests, as your name suggests.

February 1998

Translation Rana Dasgupta

Notes

1. Marie Darrieussecq, *Naissance des fantômes*, P. O. L., Paris, 1998, p. 150.
2. *Ibid.*, p. 152.

The Sorceress Philippe Sollers

After You, Dearest Photography: Reflections on the Work of Francesca Woodman

David Levi Strauss

> "Everything comes down, in the final analysis, to taking account
> of the relations of light which, from the point of view of knowledge,
> should perhaps be considered in its very simplest details."
>
> André Breton, *L'Amour fou*

> "Because time is out there, eaten by light."
>
> Norma Cole, "Spinoza in Her Youth," unpublished poem

The first photograph we have, in time, is a self-portrait of the

artist at age thirteen. It already displays the gestural clarity and emotional depth that will drive the work to come. Francesca Woodman sits sideways on a sort of pew, her head turned toward the camera and tilted forward, bowing, so that her hair ("fair-tressed Ariadne") hangs down over her face which is further obscured by shadow. She is dressed in a heavy cable-knit sweater and jeans. Her right elbow rests on the pew's arm so that her right hand hangs suspended in light, relaxed and expressive, while her left hand is tensed and extended to grasp the cable release, stretched taut to the camera. The cable (or rod?) widens as it nears the lens, forming a black dagger shape that cuts diagonally back toward the sitter. That enhanced line represents both release and bondage, bridge and tether: Ariadne's thread.

The constitutive facts of Francesca Woodman's life are by now well known. We know that she was born in 1958, the daughter of artists George and Betty Woodman, that she began taking photographs seriously at age thirteen or fourteen and continued this involvement into her twenty-second year, building up, in this brief time, a remarkably coherent and affecting body of work. And we know that on January 19, 1981, just two and a half months before her twenty-third birthday, she took her own life, leaping from a window on the Lower East Side in Manhattan to her death.

This latter fateful knowledge cannot help but influence the way we view her art. Because they are photographs, "evidence of a novel kind," our projections are inevitable. As Barthes and others have pointed out, paintings and drawings are iconic, while photographs are indexical; that is, they always point to something else. Woodman's images are haunted, as all photographs are, by death, but these harbor additional ghosts.[1] Because they are self-portraits of a particular kind, we scrutinize them for clues to their untimely cessation. But we would be missing a great deal of substance if we confined our viewing of these images to an overly forensic search for a *corpus delicti*.

From the beginning, Francesca Woodman's relation to the camera was intense, never casual. She did not take the transformations it wrought lightly (becoming an image is a secret process, a mystery). Recognizing right away that this "mirror with a memory" could be the stage for an inquiry, she organized her work into etudes, exercises, and experiments—what Rosalind Krauss termed in her essay on the work "problem sets."[2] Often responses to specific assignments in school, these sets in time became a working method. The artist remarked on the origin of this method in a notebook entry: "What happened is that I played the piano for a long time. The pieces I played most were themes on variations, Scarlatti, etc. This occurs in my imagery." And in a series produced in Providence in 1976 and 1977 when Woodman was a student at the Rhode Island School of Design, the musical model is made explicit.

An image of her nude figure crouched and bowing before a scarred wall, with a torn sheet of wallpaper covering her back like a shell, and her hands caressing the wall like a keyboard, is captioned, "Then at one point I did not need to translate the notes; they went directly into my hands." Another remarkable self-portrait shows her dressed in a black brocade gown opened to reveal one breast. The upper edge of the frame cuts off her head at the chin, which is balanced on the right by a compensatory piece of white lace hanging down into the frame. Under the image is scrawled, "When i started again" (this line appears under erasure, obscured by a brushstroke) "i could no longer play. i could not play by instinct." From her right hand dangles a small knife with a curved blade, in motion, and from a cut under the line of her breast emerges a strip of photo-booth self-portraits, spattered with real or simulated blood. No longer playing by instinct, her body has become an automatic producer of images that issue from a self-induced wound. All she needed to do, for the images to come, was open the wound.

In an image from the same time, the artist/model sits on the edge of a white chair, wearing only a pair of black shoes. She is seen from the waist down, and before her on the floor is a shadowgraph, the negative impression her prone body has made in white powder, mimicking the impression light makes on silver salts. In another, she kneels on a heavily framed mirror placed flat on the floor. Her head and upper body are in motion, so that her face is distorted, and only her legs and one hand are in focus. And in the series titled *A Woman/A Mirror/A Woman Is a Mirror for a Man*, that same heavy mirror, now stood upright in a corner of the studio and tilted in its frame, is again the ground for her actions. She turns away from it, embraces it, gazes into it, and, in the final image, places herself awkwardly between it and a sheet of glass—between transparency and reflection—in an attempt to flatten herself into a complete image. Or perhaps she is attempting to go back through the looking-glass, into a world before the fall into representation and self-consciousness, before the gendered mirror-stage, before the wounds of image-making and being made into an image have been inflicted.

In a single image related to the *House* series of 1975-76, the artist appears as Alice, in a Victorian-looking dress. She looks directly into the camera and gestures oddly with her hands and arms toward a door ajar, drawing it open to the darkness beyond, the seductive *camera obscura*.

"Now we come to the passage. You can just see a little *peep* of the passage in Looking-Glass House, if you leave the door of our drawing-room wide open: and it's very like our passage as far as you can see, only you know it may be quite different on beyond."[3]

Because of Woodman's age when these works were made (thirteen to twenty-two), it would be retroactively premature to try to place them definitively in the context of other work being done in photography at the time. In her feminist reading of Woodman's work, Abigail Solomon-Godeau calls it the work of a prodigy, noting that "prodigies in photography are singularly rare; women prodigies virtually unheard of."[4] Growing up with artist parents and friends, Woodman knew a great many things about how art happens that young artists often spend half a lifetime discovering (or rediscovering): that seeing and making are not the same thing, that making has a logic of its own that must be attended to, that ideas are cheap and embodiment dear, that art is the labor in the process of creation, that life is short but art is long. Consequently, her youthful work is not a series of false starts and forays, but rather the substantially realized fragments of a whole that was defeated by time. This was a real inquiry, however incomplete.

That said, it remains the work of youth and inexperience. And as such, as both Solomon-Godeau and Krauss asserted in their introduction of Woodman's work to the public in 1986, it is difficult to place this work in the chronology of the institution of art photography (Krauss uses the term "Straight Photography"). But I believe Solomon-Godeau too quickly dismisses its connection to the one tradition it can usefully be placed in relation to: surrealist photography.[5] It is not, after all, so great a distance from the bookstore called *Humanité* in Paris, to the one called *Maldoror* in Rome.

The relation of Woodman's work to surrealist photography is not primarily one of style, although its focus on transformations and deformations of the female nude, its attraction to romantic ruins and dilapidated interiors, and its use of fetish and found objects ("those object-talismans surrealism still cares so much about"[6])—gloves, swans, umbrellas, costume jewelry, and mirrors—are surrealist tropes, and a number of single works (such as the "explosante-fixe" before the wall in Rome) and sets (such as the "veiled-erotic" of *Horizontale/Verticale*) could almost have been made by Man Ray or Lee Miller. But by the time Woodman stopped making photographs, surrealist style had been thoroughly absorbed into the "corporate surrealism" of product advertising and fashion photography, where desire is downsized into consumer choice. Surrealist *style* had already become a cliché.

Woodman's work participates not so much in the surrealist style as in its substance, its original revolutionary desire to crack the code of appearances and see through the looking-glass. As Rosalind Krauss has shown, photography and surrealism were made for each other. In her essay on "Photography in the Service of Surrealism," Krauss writes that surrealist photography "exploits the very special connection to reality with which all photography is endowed. Photography is an imprint or transfer of the real; it is a photochemically processed trace causally connected to that thing in the world to which it refers in a way parallel to that of fingerprints or footprints or the rings of water that cold glasses leave on tables."[7] Surrealists recognized photography's subversive potential in their assault on bourgeois values and reality, and on Straight Photography's narrow sense of realism.

"Contrivance," writes Krauss, "is what ensures that a photograph will seem surrealist." In not admitting of "the natural, as opposed to the cultural or made," surrealist photography insisted on the utter constructedness of the real, including the categories of identity: "Within surrealist photographic practice, too, *woman* was in construction, for she is the obsessional subject there as well. And since the vehicle through which she is figured is itself manifestly constructed, *woman* and *photograph* become figures for each other's condition: ambivalent, blurred, indistinct, and lacking in, to use Edward Weston's word, 'authority.'"[8]

In Francesca Woodman's work, we see a young woman making it up (photography) from the beginning, recognizing no authority outside of her intimate relationship to the camera, and claiming no authority outside the frame of her photographs. This is a scandal in the house of Straight Photography. Whereas photographs most often trace the relation between the one photographing and the one photographed, in Woodman's images that relation is collapsed. The result is not the closed circuit of narcissism (which all women photographing themselves are accused of inhabiting), since it always imagines an other, a viewer outside (space and time). The playful eroticism of the odalisques is neither narcissism nor deconstruction of the male gaze, since these images are clearly directed outward, to an other. This other—whether an individual or the camera—is actually the Narcissus to Woodman's Echo. When Woodman looks in the mirror, she is looking in the mirror *for the camera,* which is us, since the camera is our temporal representative. Given the fact that cameras have most often been in the hands of men who want to look at women, a beautiful young woman handling her own camera is always a subversion.

Krauss locates the concept of "convulsive beauty" at the very core of the surrealist aesthetic, a concept that she says "reduces to an experience of reality transformed into representation." And in his *L'Amour fou,* Breton asks "that we look for a new beauty, a beauty 'envisaged exclusively to produce passion,'" and describes the operations of convulsive beauty in characteristically uncompromising terms: "There can be no beauty at all, as far as I am concerned—convulsive beauty—except at the cost of affirming the reciprocal relations linking the object seen in its motion and in its repose."[9]

Over and over in Francesca Woodman's photographs, the body—her own body—is caught at that precise point where motion becomes repose, where a fleeting gesture settles onto paper. Often the body is in motion while another object of focus (a mirror, a wall, a bolt of fabric, or a basin coiled with eels) is seen at rest. Or one body is in motion while another rests (in the vitrines of *Space²* or the studio of *Charlie the Model*).

Woodman's *Charlie the Model* series is a moving meditation on the exigencies of representation. In the beginning, an affable middle-aged man stands in for the artist, giving her a chance to reflect on the condition of being turned into a photograph from the other side of the camera (later, she cannot resist joining Charlie on stage, leaving her friend Sloan Rankin to release the shutter). In the first image, Charlie the model, dressed in a white T-shirt and slacks, holds a sheet of glass in front of him and looks into the mirror, on which is written his name. Under this print the artist has written "Charlie has been a model at RISD for 19 years. i guess he knows a lot about being flattened to fit paper." In this image appear three different modulators representing three elements of transformation: a sheet of glass (transparency), a mirror (reflectivity), and a window (illumination). Charlie stands in the corner formed by the wall with the window and the wall with the mirror. He holds the sheet of glass before him like a frame and leans into the mirror, forming a body bridge between window and mirror. Camera, mirror, corner, and window delineate a square that is rotated ninety degrees from the focal plane. In the last image in the series, Charlie sits on the floor nude, with his legs spread, holding the sheet of glass pressed awkwardly against his body. It flattens him. He closes his eyes and leans back against the mirror, in defeat. The caption reads "Sometimes things seem very dark. Charlie had a heart attack. I hope things get better for him." Becoming an image (being "flattened to fit paper") points toward death. And we are all becoming images.

The manipulation of photographic space that Woodman explores in this series and elsewhere is sophisticated and clear, but I find her attempts to manipulate time even more compelling. These attempts reached an apogee in Woodman's last images for the *Temple Project* in New York in the Spring of 1980. In one of these studies we see two female nudes, stripped bare to the waist and holding shallow fabric-covered boxes over their heads. The slight movement of the boxes causes a blur from the bottom of the frame to the top, so that our eye moves up the image and across to the left, in a way that implies a whole row of caryatides. Somehow, this contrived and otherwise banal image manages to move outside of time, evoking those archaic column-shafts in the shape of draped women of the Athenian Erechtheum, or the earlier (late sixth-century B.C.) Siphnian Treasury at Delphi. These figures represent priestesses of Artemis Caryatis, who presided over female rites of passage, especially the transition from *parthenos* (virgin) to *gyne* (fully acculturated woman).[10] Woodman saw something in these figures that allowed her to simulate them photographically. Just as the ancient caryatides were a way to bring the female figure into space as an architectural element, Woodman's photograph casts these figures into time, into a participation in the archaic.

Even more intriguing is another study for the *Temple Project* showing a wall in a bathroom: peeling paint over an ornate tile border, a sliver of a mirror, a round metal armature of some kind on a glass shelf, and a glass towel rod on which a white silk garment is wound in regular spirals. This bathroom could be in Pompeii. This image, too, is *out of time* in its archaic resonance.

Perhaps Francesca Woodman was herself out of time, exiled in the present. In her photographs, she materialized her condition and transformed it, manipulating appearances in order to move around in time. In her last images, for the *Temple Project,* she accomplished this to an extraordinary degree. Perhaps it was not enough. Or perhaps the transformation continues undiminished, for she is here now, in her images.

Notes

The title refers to a line by Breton's *Introduction au discours sur le peu de réalité* that Walter Benjamin quotes in his 1929 essay on surrealism: "Quietly. I want to pass where no one yet has passed, quietly!—After you, dearest language."

1. "All those young photographers who are at work in the world, determined upon the capture of actuality, do not know that they are agents of Death. [...] Contemporary with the withdrawal of rites, Photography may correspond to the intrusion, in our modern society, of an asymbolic Death, outside of religion, outside of ritual, a kind of abrupt dive into literal Death. *Life / Death*: the paradigm is reduced to a simple click, the one separating the initial pose from the final print." Roland Barthes, *Camera Lucida: Reflections on Photography*, trans. Richard Howard, New York, Hill and Wang, 1981, p. 92.

2. Rosalind Krauss, "Problem Sets," in *Francesca Woodman: Photographic Work*, catalog for the first showing of Woodman's work at the Wellesley College Museum and Hunter College Art Gallery in 1986.

3. Lewis Carroll, *Through the Looking-Glass, and What Alice Found There*, London, Macmillan and Co., 1872, p. 10.

4. Abigail Solomon-Godeau, "Just Like a Woman," in *Francesca Woodman: Photographic Work, op.cit.*, p. 14.

5. *Ibid.*, p. 36: "Certain correspondences or similarities that one might note between Surrealist photographs and Woodman's work are most likely fortuitous."

6. André Breton, *Mad Love*, English translation of *L'Amour fou* by Mary Ann Caws, Lincoln and London, University of Nebraska Press, 1987, p. 101.

7. Rosalind Krauss, "Photography in the Service of Surrealism," in Rosalind Krauss and Jane Livingston, *L'Amour fou: Photography & Surrealism*, Washington, D.C. and New York, The Corcoran Gallery of Art and Abbeville Press, 1985, p. 31.

8. Rosalind Krauss, "Corpus Delicti," *ibid.*, p. 95.

9. André Breton, *Mad Love, op. cit.*, p. 10. In her note on this passage, translator Mary Ann Caws sets out a serviceable genealogy of the surrealist aesthetic: "As cubism can be thought to be the picturing of an object many times from many angles of repose, and futurism to be the picturing of it in action, surrealism combines the two tendencies."

10. İn Homer, Artemis is also a death-bringing deity who brings sudden death to women as Apollo does to men. When Odysseus addressed the shade of his mother in the Underworld, he asked her, "What fate of grievous death overcame thee? Was it long disease, or did the archer, Artemis, assail thee with her gentle shafts, and slay thee?" (*Odyssey*, XI: 171-3)

Original contact sheet, Italy, 1977-1978, detail

Francesca Woodman hanging her photographs for the exhibition *Cinque Giovani Artisti*
Galleria Ugo Ferranti, Rome, Italy, June 1978

IMMAGINI
FRANCESCA WOODMAN
LIBRERIA MALDOROR
VIA DE PARIONE, 41
MARZO 20 - 30

Sig. P.
Missoyi
Maldoror
Via de Parioni 41
Roma

Invitation to the first solo exhibition of Francesca Woodman at the *Maldoror* bookshop
including an original contact print, Rome, Italy, 20-30 March 1978

Un séjour romain
Elizabeth Janus

"The aesthetic is so intense that you feel you should live in the taste of it,
should extract the nutritive essence of the atmosphere. For positively it's *such* an atmosphere!
The weather is perfect, the sky as blue as the most exploded tradition fames it,
the whole air glowing and throbbing with lovely color."

Henry James, "From a Roman Notebook," in *Italian Hours*

If the artist's pilgrimage to Rome has become mostly a cliché,

the experience of the city for even the most cynical traveler still elicits a sense of awe at not only the historical depth of a place but that it can remain so vital, so real, and, as Henry James wrote more than a hundred years ago, such an "aesthetic luxury." When Francesca Woodman arrived in Rome in 1977 as a 19-year-old art student from the Rhode Island School of Design (RISD) in Providence, she already had a sense of Italy as she had spent many summers and a year of primary school in Tuscany, where her parents own a house. She spoke Italian fluently and unlike the other American students who had come for the academic year on an honors program at RISD's Roman affiliate, she integrated easily into the city's fabric. As many who met her at the time recall, she moved easily throughout Rome, constantly absorbing its energy, its visual splendors and contrasts, and particularly its quality of light. The photographs that Woodman took there, between the spring of 1977 and the summer of 1978, all bear witness to the fact that she had found an environment—one of history, of classicism, of sensuality, and of decay—that seemed to have been well suited to her artistic sensibility. Already in Providence she was photographing herself in interiors visibly marked by age and neglect, such as the photographs *House #3* or *Space*[2], both from 1975-1976. In Rome, this became even more evident, particularly in a series of four photographs called *Self-Deceit* (1978), taken in the basement of RISD's 15th-century building, the palazzo Cenci, but also in the *Angel* series, which was partially conceived in Providence and finally realized in Rome.

In retrospect, Woodman's year in Rome seems to have been crucial to the flourishing of her art, partly because of the effects the city's historical and artistic significance as well as its physical beauty had on her, but also because it offered her the freedom to work as an artist rather than an art student. The Rhode Island School of Design's Honors Program in Rome was set up in 1960 to allow the best students from its American campus to spend a year abroad, traveling throughout Italy and Europe and working independently on their art. The school requires that students attend weekly art history lectures and two week-long tours—of northern and of southern Italy—but apart from these general requirements, they are allowed almost total freedom to work as they wish. Periodic critiques with the program's director give students feedback on how their work is evolving and at the time Woodman was in Rome, she also came into contact with photographers like Aaron Siskind who, along with Harry Callahan, had taught in RISD's photography department.

This freedom was important for Woodman because although she had already produced a significant and unusually mature body of work in Providence (one that prefigured many of the concerns that would be addressed by women photographers in the United States during the 1980s, particularly the privileging of female subjectivity and an interrogation into the representation of the female body), in Rome, she concentrated more intensely on expanding and developing her ideas and creative impulses outside of obligatory school exercises. Unlike most of the RISD students who stayed in a *pensione* near the school,

Woodman and her friend, fellow student, and occasional model, Sloane Rankin, rented an apartment about ten minutes away on the via dei Coronari in the piazza San Salvatore in Lauro, a neighborhood near the piazza Navona that had attracted artists for centuries (Benvenuto Cellini and Caravaggio had lived nearby and Cy Twombly's apartment on the via Monserrato was on Woodman's frequent walks from school to home). Around the corner and next to the mercato della Pace, where she often bought food, Woodman discovered the *Libreria Maldoror,* a small bookshop run by two young bibliophiles, Giuseppe (Cristiano) Casetti and Piero Missigoi. Opened in 1977, the *Maldoror* became a point of attraction for many young artists and intellectuals during its short period of existence (it closed in 1981). It was a place where one could find an eclectic array of books, catalogues, journals, vintage postcards and photographs, from early 20th-century medical textbooks and books on magic to old exhibition catalogues. The major interests of Casetti and Missigoi were those writers and artists associated with Symbolism, Surrealism, and Futurism, as well as others who, since the end of World War II, had been ignored or had come to be considered reactionary or in some way connected with fascism. It was a place where one could find first-edition books and catalogues by and about André Breton, Isidore Ducasse, Odilon Redon, Balthus, Antonin Arthaud, Georges Bataille, Louis-Ferdinand Céline and Friedrich Nietzsche, or examples of the Italian revue *Sapere,* which just before the war published fascist propaganda next to articles by the artist and writer, Alberto Savinio, brother of Giorgio de Chirico. In fact, it was in one issue of *Sapere* that Woodman likely saw an article and series of photographs by a Hungarian scientist who claimed to have invented a "disappearing machine". The pictures show a hand gradually growing fainter from one frame to the next and then disappearing completely. Later found to be a hoax and renounced by the publishers, the pictures remain a fascinating *exposé* on photographic manipulation and bear a remarkable similarity to certain of Woodman's own photographs, including the *Angel* series, which expanded on her interest in photographically capturing transparency.

The late 1970s in Italy, as in much of the rest of Europe, was a time of political and social upheaval. The Italian Communist Party had been given a voice in the government for the first time in its existence after a 1976 *compromesso storico* or "historic compromise" which was an accord struck between its secretary general, Enrico Berlinguer, and the Christian Democrat premier, Aldo Moro. Student unrest and leftist idealism dominated the political landscape with constant student protests, the omnipresence of police, and frequent clashes between the two. It was in this climate that the proclaimed apolitical stance of *Maldoror* came to be seen, at best, as an extraordinary, even anarchistic, presence in Rome due to its defiance of the prevalence and rigidity of leftist dogma; or, at worst, it was seen as a bookstore with right-wing leanings. This controversial non-conformism was for many young artists and intellectuals its greatest attraction. Woodman was so taken with the bookstore that in January 1978 she asked if the owners would consider showing some of her photographs there. As she was to do frequently, rather than make the proposal directly to

Casetti and Missigoi, she sent a postcard from Tuscany that was addressed to Casetti's dog, Ducasse, in which she asked him to convince his master to organize an exhibition of her photographs in the basement of the bookshop, which often served as a small gallery. Four days before Woodman's exhibition was to open at *Maldoror* on the 20th of March 1978, Aldo Moro was kidnapped in Rome by the Red Brigades. It was a day remembered as one of silence, of suspended animation, of disbelief, and of fear, but neither this event nor Moro's assassination three months latter, seemed to have had significant effect on Woodman, who like many Americans remained at a comfortable distance from politics and its repercussions.

In Casetti, Missigoi, and the artist Sabina Mirri (who at the time was living with Missigoi), Woodman had found interlocutors who were as passionate about books as she was about her art and discussions with the three were constant as was the continuous exchange of ideas. At *Maldoror* she discovered not only Breton and the Surrealists, but the Italian geometry notebook that she used as support for her 1981 artist's book *Some Disordered Interior Geometries*, which is dedicated to Casetti, Missigoi and Mirri. She also saw early 20th-century medical textbooks, often with strangely colored photographic illustrations of human disease. In one from 1914, the *Trattato di medicina legale,* is the reproduction of a small black and white photograph of a mirror covered with vertical black streaks, which, though a beautiful image, is in fact a morbid document of a suicide victim who had slit his throat. Though it is not certain that Woodman knew this photograph (Piero Missigoi suggests that it is very likely he showed it to her), it is remarkably similar to two of the most powerful images that Woodman produced during that year. In one, her naked torso is bent backwards toward the camera, her mouth open as if screaming, and in the other, her blurred, marked body is shown halfway outside of the right frame—both figures being set against a wall covered with blood-like streaks of paint.

Her conversations with the owners of *Maldoror*, as well as with another frequent visitor to the bookshop, the Rome-based American artist and critic, Edith Schloss, focused on art more than on literature. Besides the Futurists and Surrealists, she discovered their precursors, such as the Viennese Symbolist Max Klinger, who was an important influence on De Chirico and whose series of etchings from 1881, *Paraphrase über den Fund eines Handschuhs (Fantasies on the Finding of a Glove)*, may have inspired several of the images that Woodman included in *Some Disordered Interior Geometries*.

Her friendship with Sabina Mirri was to develop into a close one and it remained strong even after Woodman returned to the United States. They were constant companions in Rome and went almost daily to the Campo dei Fiori, a well-known market near the villa Farnese that was halfway between school and her apartment. There she bought the flowers and old clothes that often found their way into her photographs, as did the fish and eels or *capitone*—a Roman Christmas tradition—that she found at the market in piazza Vittorio. Through Woodman's friendship with Sabina Mirri, she was also introduced to Mirri's fellow painters, a group of young artists—Giuseppe Gallo, Gianni Dessì, and Bruno

Ceccobelli—who had set up studios in an abandoned spaghetti factory on via degli Ausoni in the neighborhood of San Lorenzo near the train station and not far from the university.

The general mood among artists at the time was one of transition, from the omnipresence of Minimalism and Conceptual art to the pleasures and poetry of painting. As one example of a sign of the times the *mostra* of the 1978 Venice Biennale, organized by Achille Bonito Oliva, featured all those major artistic tendencies from America and Europe that characterized the moment: pre-Pop and Pop art, Arte Povera and Conceptual, Minimal and Land art. But while the Biennale may have represented the established art scene, in Rome the first signs of painting's rebirth were already visible in the work of Francesco Clemente, Enzo Cucchi, Sandro Chia—the artists who would be grouped by Bonito Oliva, in 1980, under the term *transavanguardia* and whose neo-romantic paintings would dominate much of that decade.[1]

Woodman spent many hours at a building on via degli Ausoni, in an unheated, fifth-floor space just above the studio of Giuseppe Gallo, with whom she became very close. On one particularly cold January afternoon, Gallo found her naked and trembling with cold, waiting for the proper light in which to photograph herself. Gallo and the other young artists in his circle saw Woodman as a "curious" phenomenon, constantly working and thinking about her photographs, very self-confident, determined, ambitious, and with a passion and intensity that was rare for her age; but at the same time, she was seen as extremely sensitive and tender—a duality that may have translated into certain of her photographs. She was rarely seen without her camera and tripod, even when going out with friends to the bar *Fassi*, a dilapidated 19th-century restaurant in the north of Rome, where they often gathered to eat and talk. And in the spring of 1978, it was Gallo who suggested to the art dealer Ugo Ferranti that he include Woodman in an exhibition of young Romans that was being organized for the following June. For Woodman, the show was an important professional leap from the small basement exhibition she had done three months earlier at *Maldoror*, but as was noted by several friends, it was not a pleasant experience, given Ferranti's reputedly difficult character and his well-known preference for male artists.

Caught between the poetics of painting and the passion for books, Woodman's stay in Rome was characterized by constant intellectual stimulation and a warm, specifically Italian, sense of familiarity. After returning to the United States, in the summer of 1978, she corresponded with several of her friends there over the next two years, often mentioning how much her year in Rome had meant to her. In December 1979 she wrote to Edith Schloss from Providence: "I miss Rome extra these days [...] I think about them [Casetti and Missigoi] too [...] and have been reading a lot of those futurist books and related stuff." And later, from New York in May 1980: "I was homesick for Italy this winter for months and spent all my time reading in Italian and hanging out with some really idiotic little gigolos only for the pleasure of the purity of their Italian accents..." and "It's funny how while I was living in Italy the culture there didn't effect me that much and now I have all this fascination with the architecture, etc." In another letter from New York in September 1980 to Sabina Mirri she writes "I would like to go back to Italy. The only problem is that the art world here forgets you if you leave for five minutes."

The difficulties of being a young artist in New York, which were contrary to the more supportive atmosphere of her coterie in Italy, were obvious to Woodman and the dog-eats-dog competition of the New York art scene doubtlessly effected her memories of Rome. However, the significance of that year was tangible in that her experience of the art and architecture of the place translated into one of the last projects that she did before she died, what she called *The Temple Project*. In the photographs from this series Woodman attempted to recreate the caryatids from classical architecture, using real women as columns and marble slabs as capitals; in essence, turning female form as functional structure into living flesh. Woodman's Roman year was, if anything, an important period of self-recognition and intellectual stimulation. It might also be considered the moment when she realized that others finally understood what she seemed to have known all along: that she was an artist.

Notes

1. "This movement considers language, or visual expression, to be an instrument of transition and the means for passing from one work to another and from one style to another. Avant-gardism, in all its various forms after the Second World War, develops according to an evolutionistic principle called linguistic Darwinism whose roots are to be found in historic avant-gardisms. Transavant-gardism, on the other hand, operates beyond these fixed coordinates and follows a nomadic scheme based on the reversibility of all past languages [...]; dematerialization and detachment have been replaced by a preference for manual creativity and the pleasure derived from this kind of painting has restored traditional values."
Achille Bonito Oliva in *Genius Loci,* exhibition catalogue, Florence, 1980, n.p.

Recto of the letter Francesca Woodman sent to Yellen Associates,
MacDowell Colony, Peterborough, New Hampshire, 13 July 1980

Dear Bet + Golen,   July 15, 1980
        It's very nice here and most of my projects
going well. They have a big darkroom + studio for that
that has everything even a color enlarge which I wish
I knew how to use... On the reverse side you see
francesca thinking about Birch trees, with I see
small success but todays project is going much better. I've
never had 24 hrs a day to work undisturbed before
with lunch + linens brought and wild strawberries growing out
back. It makes me feel very privileged, very spoiled. When
i come back you must come to dinner on 17th St— that
would please me so much.   XXXX Francesca
                Macdowell Colony, Peterborough NH 03458

Yellen Associates-
838 Ave of America
+29th St.
NY-NY.

RETURN TO SENDER
ARTICLE TOO SMALL
NON-MAILABLE

Verso of the letter Francesca Woodman sent to Yellen Associates,
MacDowell Colony, Peterborough, New Hampshire, 13 July 1980

Peach Mumble—Ideas Cooking
Sloan Rankin

"Writing about Francesca Woodman is for me
like writing about my elbow. I know it well and I know how it works,
but I feel it more than I look at it."

Francesca's days were filled with events that one way or another

always became reflected in her pictures. Art and life were mirror images of each other and the transition from life to art was seamless. Nonetheless, some days were more productive than others.

The good days I experienced in Francesca's company were often based on ideas which she regularly scrawled in an old brown bonded leather ledger. In the beginning is this: "Sloan and I discussing relationship of art to state of mind, I told her to keep a journal so perhaps I should keep one myself." She also wrote that "things looked funny because my pictures depend on an emotional state....I know this is true and I thought about this for a long time. Somehow it made me feel very, very good." I had a key to wherever she lived, whether Providence, Rome or New York, where I would find the journals opened to the most recent entry, an inkwell nearby. Her fingers were ink-stained along the edges. The pages of the journal have ink smears along the edges, as do many of the photographs—all an extension of her train of thought. I never had the impression that photography was really the medium best suited for her. Most photographers prefer a dust-free neatness, but it seemed to me that Francesca was most at home in dust. (She also had a special fondness for mold.) Between the ink blots and her scrawly handwriting she jotted down her ideas by way of little sketches that often also included compositions for many of her photographs. These sketches reveal that Francesca's ideas were frequently pre-conceived and later executed with excruciating care. What the sketches do not show is the chance occurrence of light, space, and other details that were specific to the time and place of her shoots. To these less predictable or totally unpredictable encounters she reacted with spontaneity, as though it were second nature to her, an inheritance perhaps from her artistic parents who exposed her to works of art, ideas and methods, things and places of beauty throughout her childhood. Betty and George Woodman also made certain she was educated in the best art school in America.

The journals constitute an extended train of reflection about love affairs, plays on words and turns of phrase, stories heard, and the day's menu, such as "tuna fish and a lot of peach mumble. I have ideas cooking—simply need to get started working before they stick to the bottom of the pan."—a clever bit of a reminder that coached her to keep on working. She writes about the intent of her journals, which she says began as commentaries on the photographs after the photographs were taken, "a consequence of my life," as she put it, but then changed into the "primary force" for the photographs themselves, or as notations and rehearsals for the ideas we encounter in her pictures. And as she says, "That's O.K. We like a picture book."

A good day began with collecting. When she worked in her studio in an unheated room above the *Pilgrim Mills* dry goods store in Providence, she surrounded herself with her collectibles. She spent a lot of time with books, fox furs and mirrors, silk slips and patterned rayon dresses—all hung on a line of pegs Amish closet style. I regularly went on collecting sprees with Francesca, both for objects and to scout out spaces and locations for her pictures. We had the red velvet chairs that we bought delivered, but we lugged the bureau mirror-top up the stairs of *Pilgrim Mills* ourselves. In Rome we carried bags of live eels across town from piazza Vittoria, and we arranged the doors and fireplace mantles to balance on their edges for the photographs in the abandoned house on North Main street in Providence. In Rome we smuggled angel wing props past the first floor offices of the empty spaghetti factory in San Lorenzo. We pulled up *cornetti* and cappuccino in a basket to our apartment window from the bar below on the via dei Coronari, the first straight street in Rome.

Sundays we roved the city and combed the stalls at the Porta Portese flea market where we bargained for ecclesiastical garments, the sides of which we sewed up so we could wear them as dresses around the town. Bus loads of Romans scolded and hissed at us as they roared by.

In an effort to find a gallery space in New York, Hardu[1], Francesca and I carried rolls of her blueprints to the Holly Solomon Gallery in West Broadway. I was living with Mary Boone at the time, during the early years of her highly successful gallery, but Mary was showing mostly men under thirty-five and Holly was showing women as well as men. Holly gently dismissed her work as being good, but not mature enough. She said, "Come back in a couple of years."

I asked Francesca why she took off her clothes to pose and why she was so often the subject of her own photographs. "It's a matter of convenience, I'm always available," she said. The photographs and blueprints cover a wide range of subjects, but to more fully understand the nature of what she was after in her pictures, one must appreciate the tactile nature of her work—one needs to feel the texture of the surfaces and objects in the pictures against bare skin. I know this because on many occasions I was immersed in flour or some other material. And once she covered me with thick slivers of clear, cold jello in order to "outline me in neon" for a photograph.

Francesca collected people much the same way she collected props and clothes. She selected them because some aspect about them intrigued her. She had a passion for documenting her ideas and her ideas were based on things she admired, things she was obsessed with acquiring. "A lot of photography is making records of people, as objects, friends," she writes. "It is like organizing a wardrobe—in terms of size etc." As she was drawn to the tactile qualities of objects, she also was determined to somehow power the gestures and unusual features of people she encountered. One of these people was Charlie the model. Charlie was slow and deliberate and famous for saying, "Hi friend" to every passerby. He was somewhat simple minded, we thought, maybe as a result of a head injury from the war. As a model at the Rhode Island School of Design he brought to the drawing classes an enormous energy, balancing on his head or playing horse and rider with other models on his back. He was big and round. As we picked up our charcoal we all probably thought the same thing: I am about to draw a man, naked, with the biggest, roundest belly I have ever seen. For years students would flatten this three dimensional man into a two dimensional image on paper. Francesca was fascinated by this transformation. Charlie's size and disarming simplicity made her nervous, so she asked me to be present during her photographing sessions with him. As always, she was tempted to jump into the pictures herself, and within minutes Francesca was alongside Charlie, nude, playing with the cat in the studio, adjusting the mirrors, and I was now shooting pictures of the two of them.

The *Charlie* pictures were shot fast, spontaneously with elements left to chance, unlike her usual slow and composed method of working. She was not deliberate and careful, going through the mental check list as was her habit. There were other pictures taken equally fast, not obvious to the viewer unless one knew of the circumstance. For example, the one of Francesca in the front of the painted *trompe-l'œil* tomb in the church in Ravenna (Chiesa di San Francesco or Basilica di S. Appolinare Nuovo, I can't remember which), both bombed in the war, which explains the cement restoration in the lower half of the picture. The picture was taken in less than a minute. Why? Because that was all the time she had to slip out of and back into her clothes, as I once again tripped the shutter. Unfortunately we will never see the photographs she intended to make in the Museum of Natural History in New York City. One of the guards threw her out when he found her disrobing in front of one of the animal exhibits.

During our first year in college, I took a poetry class. Francesca wrote about it in her journal: "I am Sloan's ghost writer for poetry—I guess I'm glad I'm not in the poetry class alone since it is mostly my lines which come back circled in red, but I enjoy it, it gives me a chance to ruminate on things." This is a poem by Francesca Woodman, part of which became the title for a photograph:

Poem about 14 hands high

> i am apprehensive.[1] it is like when i
> played the piano.[2] first i learned to
> read music [3] and then at one point i
> no longer needed to translate the notes:
> they went directly to my hands.[4] After a
> while i stopped playing [5] and when i
> started again i found i could not
> play. i could not play by
> instinct [6] and i had forgotten how
> to read music.[7]

I did not see her during the bad days in New York, but in November 1980 she wrote me one of her last letters. It was on the back of an old photograph, not one of hers but on a portrait of three ecclesiastically clad young men, the older one holding a small book and the younger two holding lighted candles. Part of it states: "I do have standards and my life at this point is like very old coffeecup sediment and I would rather die young leaving various accomplishments, i. e. some work, my friendship with you, some other artifacts intact, instead of pell-mell erasing all of these delicate things." I remember the good days filled with wit and humor, turn of phrase and clever contradictions, the velvet, fur, tulle and taffeta-patterned days of our friendship. I remember that she could blur the distinction between the ordinary and the surreal with a tough exuberance.

Notes:

1. Editor's note: Hardu Keck, professor and director of the Honors Program of the Rhode Island School of Design in Rome from 1977 to 1978.

Peach Mumble—Ideas Cooking Sloan Rankin

RHODE ISLAND SCHOOL OF DESIGN

Providence, Rhode Island 02903

For photographing pilgrim mills

.) Keep distance in ~~the~~ photography.

A) memorial to a place aspect / photography w/ 4 X5 w/wide
Angle flowers in foreground of interior of front
door hand and wrist in foreground with rose stem lying on
it→ out side door w/ key. in studio

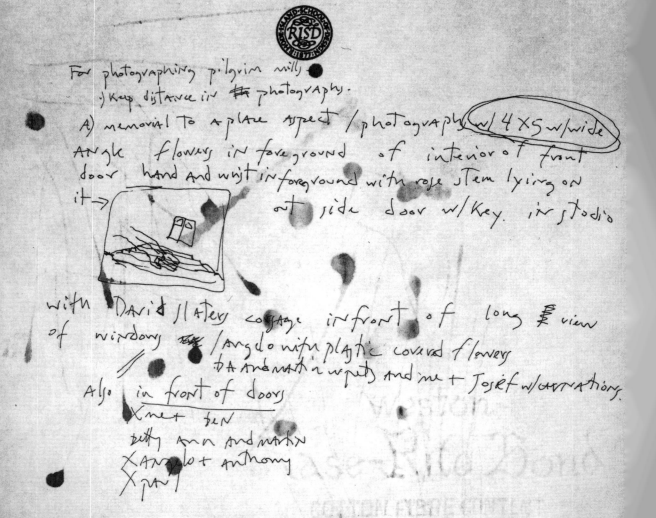

with David slaters corsage in front of long ~~&~~ view
of windows ~~also~~ / Angelo with plastic covered flowers
↓ A and martin w/ pets and me + Josef w/ carnations.

Also in front of doors
Xmet + ken
betty ann and martin
X Angelo + anthony
X paul

Extract of Francesca Woodman's diary, c. 1976-1977.

The sketch represents the entrance to her studio above the *Pilgrim Mills* shop in Providence

On Being an Angel, Providence, Rhode Island, Spring 1977, detail

Boulder, Colorado
1972-1975

Boulder, Colorado, 1972-1975

Self portrait at thirteen. Boulder, Colorado, 1972-1975

Boulder, Colorado, 1972-1975

Boulder, Colorado, 1972-1975

Boulder, Colorado, 1972-1975

Boulder, Colorado, 1972-1975

Providence, Rhode Island
1975-1978

Self portrait talking to vince. Providence, Rhode Island, 1975-1978

Providence, Rhode Island, 1975-1978

Polka Dots #5. Providence, Rhode Island, 1976-1977

Hands. Providence, Rhode Island, 1975-1978

Providence, Rhode Island, 1975-1976

Providence, Rhode Island, 1975-1978

Providence, Rhode Island, 1975-1978

Space², Providence, Rhode Island, 1975-1978

House #3. Providence, Rhode Island, 1975-1976

House #4. Providence, Rhode Island, 1975-1976

Then at one point I did not need to translate the notes: they went directly to my hands.

Providence, Rhode Island, c. 1976

From Space², Providence, Rhode Island, 1975-1976

Providence, Rhode Island, 1975-1978

Providence, Rhode Island, 1975-1978

Charlie the Model #2. #3. Providence, Rhode Island, 1976-1977

Charlie the Model #4.
There is the paper and then there is the person.
Providence, Rhode Island, 1976-1977

Charlie the Model #5.
Providence, Rhode Island, 1976-1977

Charlie the Model #6. #7. Providence, Rhode Island, 1976-1977

Charlie the Model #8. #9. Providence, Rhode Island, 1976-1977

Charlie the Model #11.
Sometimes things seem very dark. Charlie had a heart attack. I hope things get better for him.

Providence, Rhode Island, 1976-1977

Providence, Rhode Island, 1975-1976

A Woman

A Mirror

A Woman is a Mirror for a Man

Providence, Rhode Island, 1975-1978

From Space². Providence, Rhode Island, 1975-1976

From Space², Providence, Rhode Island, 1975-1976

Space². Providence, Rhode Island, 1975-1978

Space². Providence, Rhode Island, 1975-1978

Space². Providence, Rhode Island, 1975-1978

Providence, Rhode Island, 1976-1977

Sloan. Providence, Rhode Island, March 1976

Providence, Rhode Island, 1975-1978

Providence, Rhode Island, 1975-1978

Providence, Rhode Island, 1975-1976

On Being an Angel. Providence, Rhode Island, Spring 1977

On Being an Angel. Providence, Rhode Island, Spring 1977

I could no longer play
I could no play by instinct
Providence, Rhode Island, c. 1977

Providence, Rhode Island, 1976

Verticale. Providence, Rhode Island, 1976-1977

Providence, Rhode Island, 1975-1976

Horizontale. Providence, Rhode Island, 1976-1977

36. L'area d'un parallelogrammo è uguale al prodotto della base per l'altezza.

39. Il quadrato considerato qual rombo ha per superficie il semiprodotto d'una diagonale per se stessa.

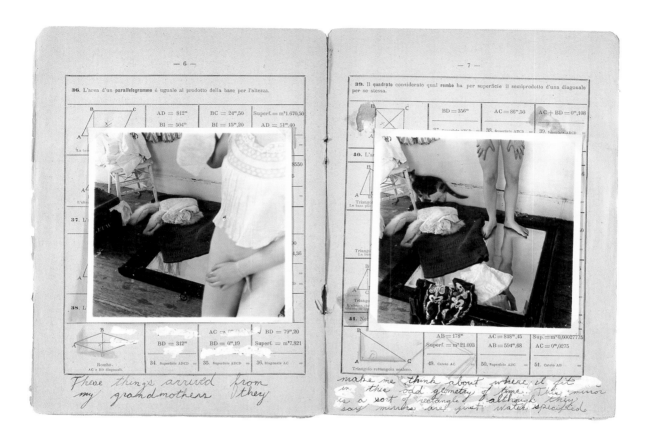

These things arrived from
my grandmothers they

make me think about where it fits
in this odd geometry of time. This mirror
is a sort of rectangle although they
say mirrors are just water specified

Some Disordered Interior Geometries. 1981, detail

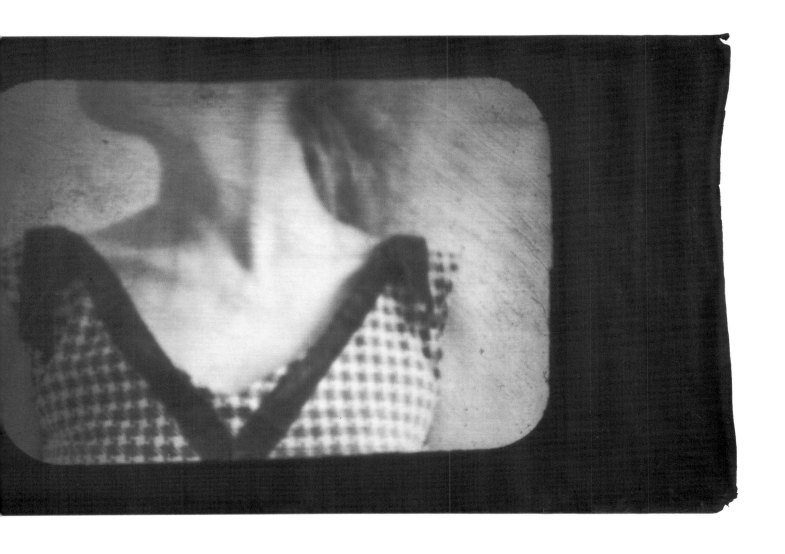

Untitled. 1980, 268 x 93,2 cm, diazotype

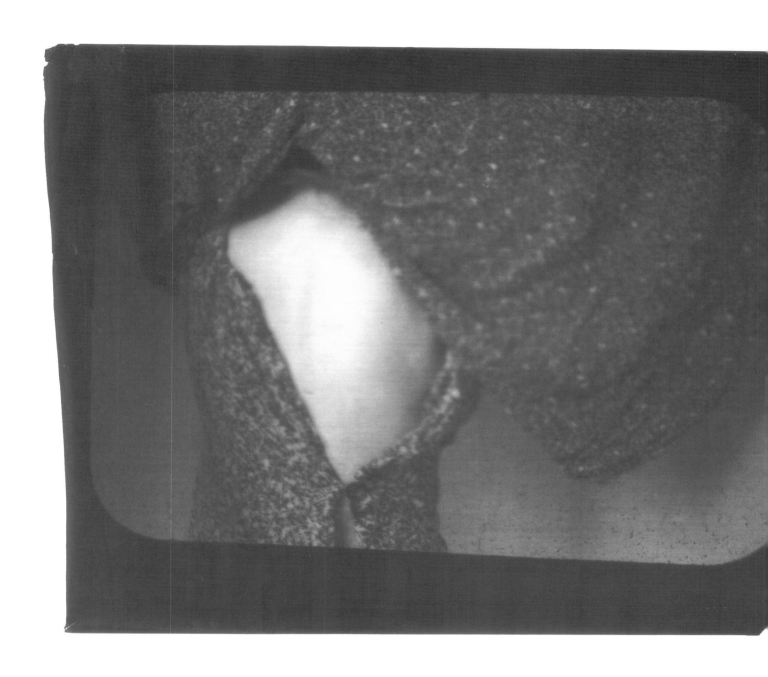

Untitled. 1980, 268 x 93,2 cm, diazotype

Zig Zag, 1980, 133 x 19,5 cm, diazotype

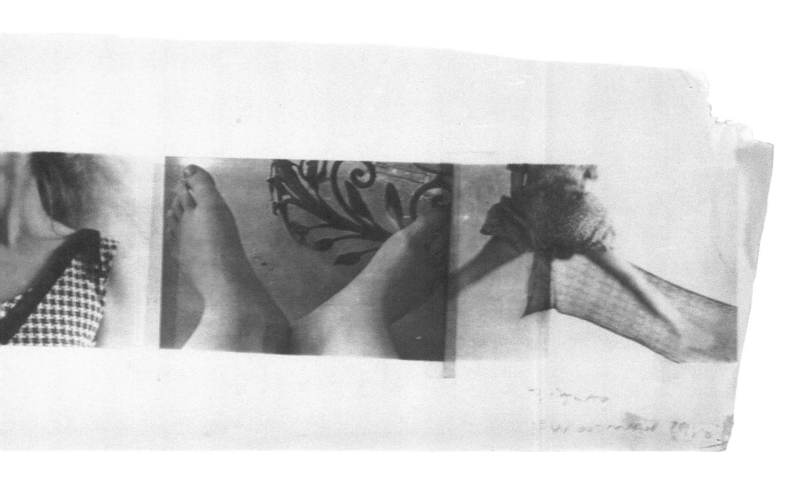

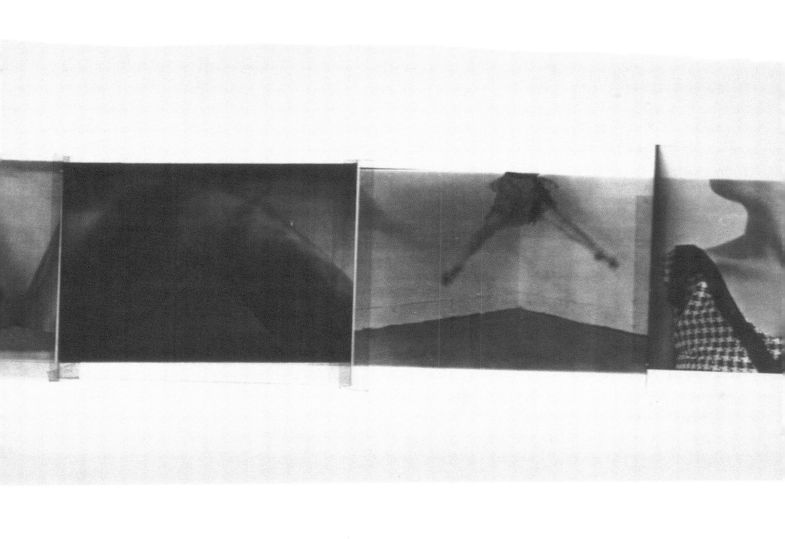

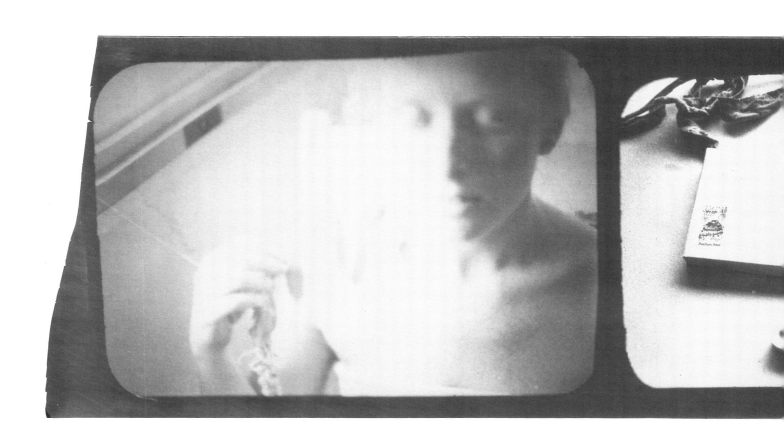

Untitled. 1980, 359 x 92,5 cm, diazotype

Untitled. 1980, 92,2 x 141,3 cm, diazotype

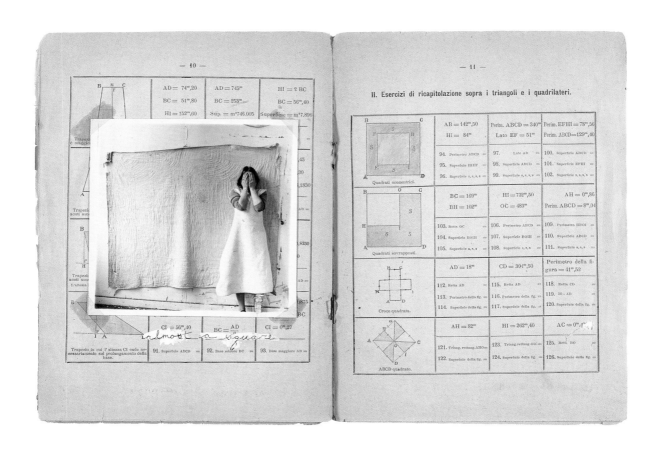

Some Disordered Interior Geometries, 1981, detail

Italy 1977-1978

Italy. May 1977-August 1978

From Angel Series. Roma, September 1977

From Angel Series, Roma, September 1977

Ravenna, Fall 1977

From Angel Series, Italy, May 1977-August 1978

Roma. May 1977-August 1978

Self-Deceit #1, Roma, 1978

Roma, May 1977-August 1978

Roma, May 1977-August 1978

Roma, May 1977-August 1978

Italy, May 1977-August 1978

Splater Plaint. Roma, May 1977-August 1978

Roma, May 1977-August 1978

Roma, May 1977-August 1978

Italy, May 1977-August 1978

Italy, May 1977-August 1978

Eel Series. Roma, May 1977- August 1978

New York 1979-1980

It must be time for lunch now, New York, 1979

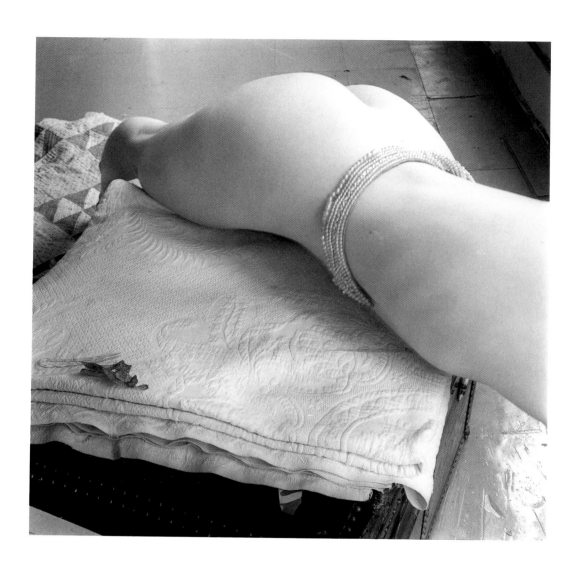

New York, 1979-1980

But lately I find a sliver of mirror is simply to slice an eye lid. New York, 1979

New York, 1979-1980

New York, 1979-1980

New York 1979-1980

New York, 1979

New York, 1979

New York, 1979

New York, 1979

New York, 1979

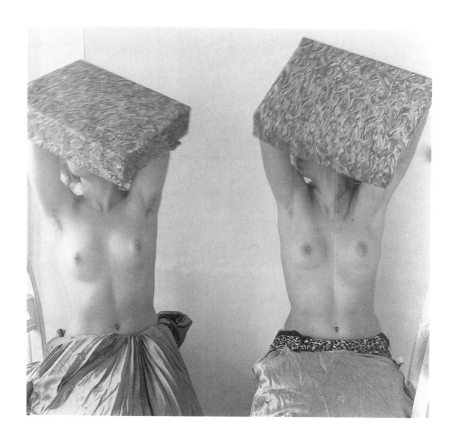

Study for Temple Project. New York, Spring 1980

Two women. one in slip. one in robe. New York, 1979

New York, 1979

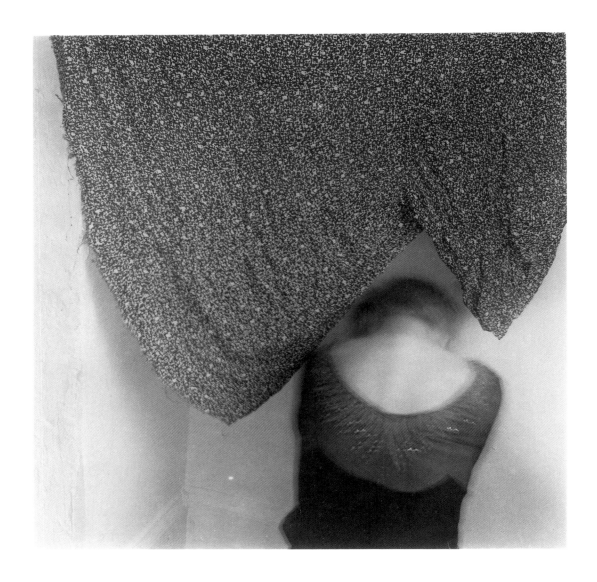

New York, 1979-1980

New York, 1980

New York, 1980

MacDowell Colony, New Hampshire
Stanwood, Washington
1979-1980

MacDowell Colony, Peterborough, New Hampshire, Summer 1980

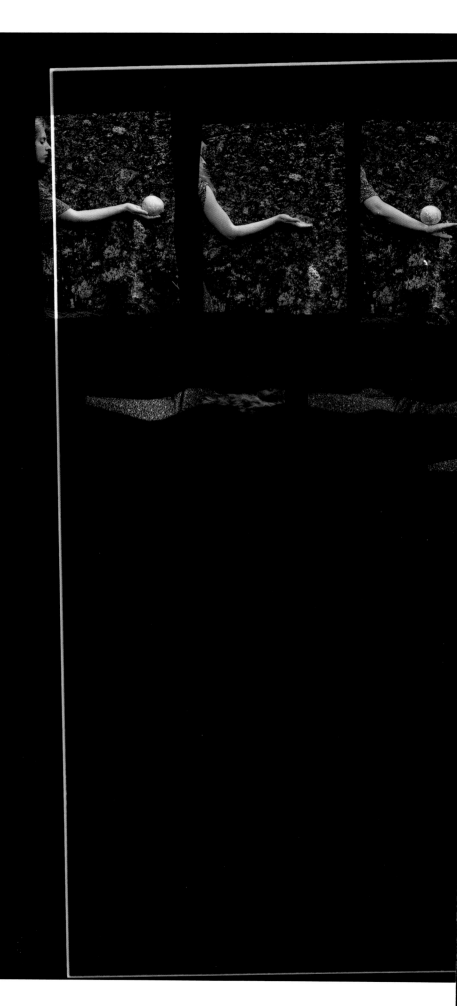

MacDowell Colony,
Peterborough,
New Hampshire,
Summer 1980

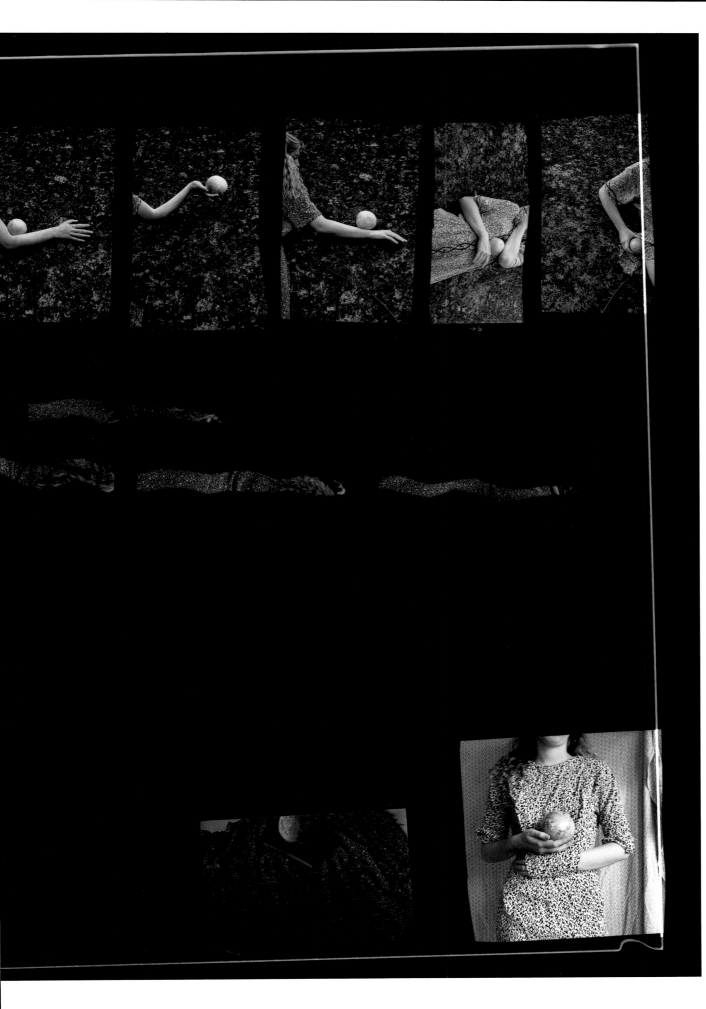

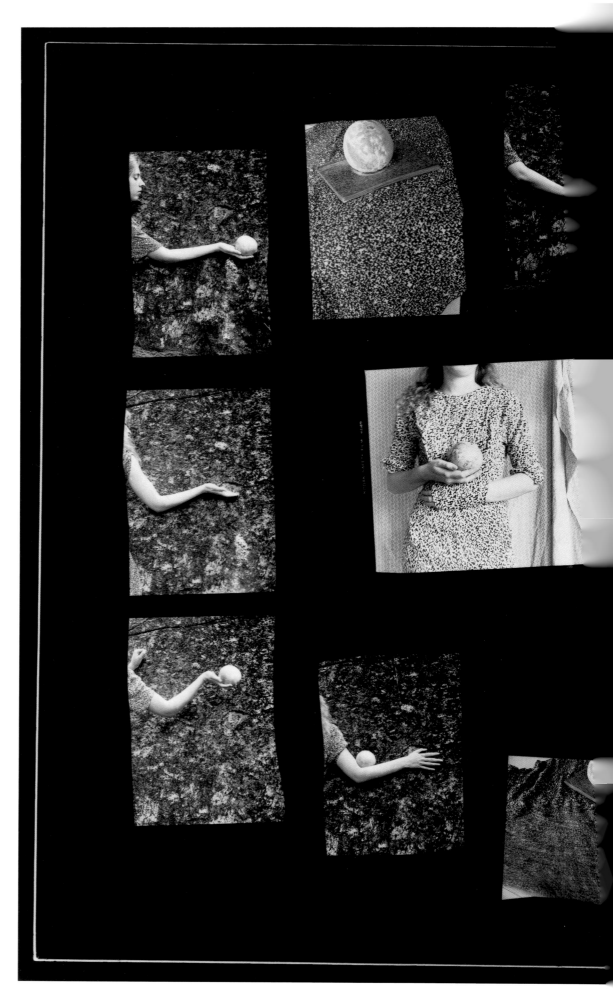

MacDowell Colony,
Peterborough,
New Hampshire,
Summer 1980

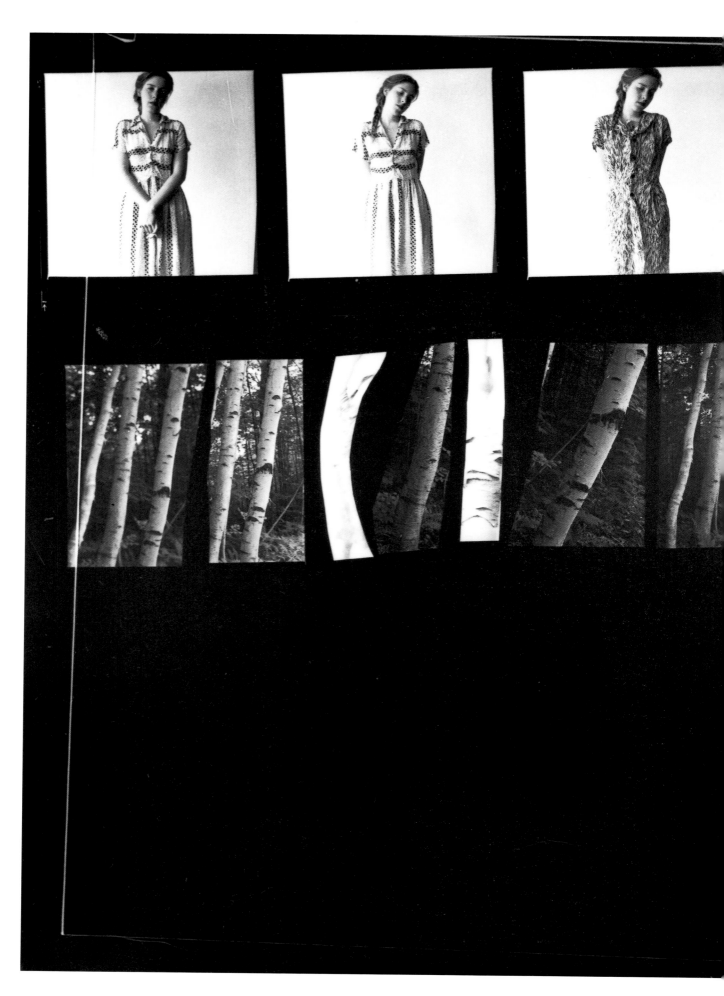

MacDowell Colony,
Peterborough,
New Hampshire,
Summer 1980

MacDowell Colony, Peterborough, New Hampshire, Summer 1980

Stanwood, Washington, Summer 1979

Stanwood, Washington, Summer 1979

Appendix

Biography

FRANCESCA WOODMAN (Denver, 1958 - New York, 1981)

Born on 3rd April 1958 in Denver, Colorado, Francesca Woodman spent most of her childhood in the university town of Boulder. Her mother was a ceramic artist and her father a painter, and Francesca grew up in her parents' workshop along with her brother Charlie. From 1963 to 1971, Francesca attended public school in Boulder and took piano lessons. When the family moved to Florence for a year in 1965, Francesca went to an Italian school. Her parents were passionate about Italy, and passed this passion on to their daughter along with her Italian first name. The family spent their summers in Antella in Tuscany, where they bought a house in 1969.

In 1972, Francesca went to Andover, Massachussets, and was admitted to the Abbott Academy boarding school, one of the rare American high schools offering art lessons. At this point in her life she was passionate about the novels of Colette. Under the guidance of one of her professors, Wendy Snyder MacNeill, she discovered photography and began to develop her skills in this area, converting her room into a photographic studio and relegating her bed to a cupboard. Her first photographs date from this time.

Francesca decided to complete her high school studies in Boulder and graduated there in June 1975. In September of the same year, she was given a place at the Rhode Island School of Design (RISD), a fine arts college in Providence. By all accounts she demonstrated, from the very beginning of her time there, an exceptional maturity and an extremely sharp understanding of her chosen field. She seems to have had an extremely strong and quite seductive personality. She found a big apartment-cum-studio to move into in the industrial building *Pilgrim Mills*. She had almost no furniture, just a few sundry objects whose texture interested her for her photography, such as animal furs, a fish bowl, some eels, a mirror, dead birds, dessert jelly... Francesca Woodman admired the work of Man Ray, Duane Michals and Weegee alias Arthur Fellig, and met Aaron Siskind who was at that time a professor at the RISD.

She persuaded her friend Sloane Rankin to leave for Rome with her to pursue the RISD's European exchange programme, taught in the sumptuous Palazzo Cenci. Francesca lived in the heart of the eternal city between May 1977 and August 1978. Inspired by the baroque sculptures decorating the city's fountains, her photography began to develop the theme of angels (*On Being an Angel*, 1977-1978). She was a frequent visitor to the gallery-bookshop *Maldoror* where she put on a solo exhibition in March 1978. She was very interested in André Breton, symbolism (particularly Max Klinger's *Fantasies on the Finding of a Glove*), and futurist photography, and in several of her letters quoted Daniel Spoerri's *An Anecdoted Topography of Chance*. She met the artists from Rome who were members of the *transavanguardia* and joined them in an exhibition at the Ugo Ferranti Gallery in June 1978.

In autumn 1978 Francesca finished her semester in Providence and graduated. In January 1979 she moved to an apartment on Second Avenue in New York City. She spent the summer in Standwood, Washington, where her boyfriend was studying. At the end of this same year, Francesca moved into a workshop on 12th Street in the East Village. She found several little jobs working as painter's model or photographer's assistant. In an attempt to make a career in photography she put together portfolios that she sent to a number of different fashion photographers, among them Deborah Turbeville whose work she had admired for some time. Her solicitations did not lead anywhere.

Francesca became artist-in-residence at MacDowell Colony, Peterborough in New Hampshire during the summer of 1980. She worked very hard, particularly at developing her photographs, taking advantage of the materials made available to the artists. She read Proust.

Back in New York, Francesca participated in several group exhibitions at the Daniel Wolf Gallery. She met critics such as Peter Frank and Max Kozloff (who drew parallels between her work and that of photographer Ralph Meatyard) and became a good friend of the surrealist art collector Timothy Baum. At the Alternative Museum of New York she exhibited her recent diazotypes, photographs printed on blue or sepia paper usually used by architects. It is this technique that she used to start work on a large-scale enterprise: the photographic reconstruction of the facade of a Greek or Roman temple that used pictures of herself and her friends as caryatids along with details from classical-style bathrooms.

In January 1981, Francesca Woodman published her *Some Disordered Interior Geometries* through Synapse Press in Philadelphia. She committed suicide on 19th January 1981.

Solo Exhibitions

1999   Centro Cultural de Belém, Lisbon, Portugal, 22 January-15 April
Centre Cultural TeclaSala, L'Hospitalet (Barcelona), Spain, 12 May-11 July
The Photographers' Gallery, London, United Kingdom, 6 August-18 September

1998   Studio Guenzani, Milan, Italy, 5 February-14 March
Galleria Dryphoto, Prato, Italy, 4 April-16 May
Fondation Cartier pour l'art contemporain, Paris, France, 11 April-31 May
Rencontres Internationales de la Photographie, Arles, France, 6 July-16 August
Kunsthal, Rotterdam, The Netherlands, 12 September-15 November

1996   Galleria Civica, Modena, Italy, 24 November 1996-9 February 1997 (exhibition catalog)

1995   Casetti Galleria Libreria, Rome, Italy, 6 December 1995-30 June 1996

1994   PaceWildensteinMacGill, New York, USA, 2 December 1994-15 January 1995

1992   *Francesca Woodman, Photographische Arbeiten*, exhibition tour: Shedhalle, Zurich, Switzerland,
31 May-26 July 1992: Westfälischer Kunstverein, Münster, Germany, 18 September-25 October 1992:
Kulturhuset, Stockholm, Sweden, 4 December 1992-7 February 1993: Suomen Valokuvataiteen
Museo SÄÄTIÖ, Helsinki, Finland, 26 March-28 April 1993: DAAD Galerie, Berlin, Germany,
8 May-13 June 1993: Galleri F15 Alby, Moss, Norway, 7 August-3 October 1993 (exhibition catalog)

1989   *Francesca Woodman, Photographic Work*, Institute of Contemporary Art, Philadelphia, USA,
14 December 1989-28 January 1990

1986   *Francesca Woodman, Photographic Work*, exhibition tour USA: Hunter College Art Gallery, New York,
13 February-14 March 1986: Wellesley College Museum, Wellesley, 9 April-8 June 1986:
University of Colorado Fine Arts Gallery, Boulder, 2 February-15 March 1987: UCI Fine Arts Gallery,
University of California, Irvine, 2 April-2 May 1987: Krannet Art Museum, Champaign, Illinois,
25 January-6 March 1988 (exhibition catalog)

1979   *Swan Song*, Woods-Gerry Gallery, Rhode Island School of Design, Providence, USA, 16-22 November

1978   Libreria Maldoror, Rome, Italy, 20-30 March

1976   Addison Gallery of American Art, Andover, USA, October

Group Exhibitions

1998   *From the Heart, The Power of Photography—A Collector's Choice, The Sondra Gilman Collection*,
        South Texas Institute of the Arts. Corpus Christi. USA. March (exhibition catalog)
        Mirror Images: Women, Surrealism and Self-Representations, exhibition tour USA: MIT,
        List Visual Arts Center. Cambridge. 10 April-28 June 1998; Miami Art Museum. Miami.
        September-December 1998; San Francisco Museum of Modern Art. San Francisco.
        February-March 1999 (exhibition catalog)

1997   *Recent Acquisitions*, Museum of Modern Art. New York. USA. 20 February-15 April
        Objectif corps, The Montreal Museum of Fine Arts. Montreal. Canada. 6 March-1 June
        Amours, Fondation Cartier pour l'art contemporain. Paris. France. 5 June-2 November
        (exhibition catalog)
        Engel, Engel, Kunsthalle Wein. Vienna. Austria. 11 June-7 September (exhibition catalog)

1996   *Inside the Visible*, exhibition tour: Institute of Contemporary Art. Boston. USA. 31 January-12 May;
        National Museum of Women in the Arts. Washington. USA. June-September;
        Whitechapel. London. United Kingdom. October-December (exhibition catalog)

1992   *Current 92: The Absent Body*, Institute of Contemporary Art. Boston. USA. 22 January-22 March
        Sprung in die Zeit, Museum für Moderne Kunst. Photographie und Architektur. Berlin. Germany.
        20 November 1992-17 January 1993 (exhibition catalog)

1989   *Vanishing Presence*, exhibition tour USA/Canada: Walker Art Center. Minneapolis.
        29 January-16 April 1989; The Detroit Institute of Art. Detroit. 9 May-2 July 1989;
        Winnipeg Art Center. Winnipeg. Canada. 27 August-22 October 1989; High Museum of Art. Atlanta.
        14 November 1989-7 January 1990; Herbert F. Johnson Museum of Art. Cornell University. Ithaca.
        30 January-27 March 1990; Virginia Museum of Fine Arts. Richmond. 22 April-17 June 1990
        (exhibition catalog)

1988   *Identity: Representation of the Self*, Whitney Museum of American Art.
        Downtown at Federal Reserve Plaza. New York. USA. 14 December 1988-10 February 1989
        Sexual Difference: Both Sides of the Camera, Wallach Art Gallery. Columbia University.
        New York. USA. 29 March-7 May

1986   *Memento Mori*, Centro Cultural de Arte Contemporáneo. Mexico City. Mexico.
        November 1986-January 1987

1980   *Pictorialism*, Daniel Wolf. Inc.. New York. USA. April
        Beyond Photography 80, The Alternative Museum. New York. USA. 19 April-17 May
        (exhibition catalog)
        Friends of the Gallery, Daniel Wolf. Inc.. New York. USA. 15 July-15 August

1978   *Group Show*, Rhode Island School of Design Gallery in Palazzo Cenci. Rome. Italy. May
        Cinque Giorani Artisti, Galleria Ugo Ferranti. Rome. Italy. 14 June-31 July

1977   *Juried Competition*, Woods-Gerry Gallery. Rhode Island School of Design. Providence. USA. March
        Photographs and Portraiture, Womanspace. Boulder. USA. April

1976   *Juried Competition*, Woods-Gerry Gallery. Rhode Island School of Design. Providence. USA. March

Bibliography

Artist's books

Some Disordered Interior Geometries, Daniel Tucker (ed.). Synapse Press. Philadelphia. 1981

Catalogs

Francesca Woodman, Galleria Civica. Modena. 1996. Text by Jen Budney

Francesca Woodman, Photographische Arbeiten/Photographic Works, catalog German/English. Shedhalle (Zurich) & Westfälischer Kunstverein (Münster). 1992. Texts by Kathrin Hixson. Harm Lux

Francesca Woodman, Photographic Work, Wellesley College Museum (Wellesley) & Hunter College Art Gallery (New York). 1986. Texts by Ann Gabhart. Rosalind Krauss. Abigail Solomon-Godeau

Articles

Brunella Antomarini. "Francesca Woodman." in *Parkett*, no. 15. Zurich. January 1988

Betsy Berne. "Francesca Woodman Remembered." in *Open City*, no. 3. New York. 1995

Anne Bertrand. "Comète." in *LimeLight*, special number. Strasbourg. June 1997

Michael Brenson. "Francesca Woodman: Photographic Work." in *The New York Times*, New York. 7 March 1986

Collective authors. "Photographs by Francesca Woodman." in *Frontiers, A Journal of Women Studies*, vol. X. no. 1. New York. 1988

Reed Glenn. "The Flowering of Francesca Woodman. A Young Photographer's Tragic Life Blooms Again in her Heart." in *Sunday Camera*, Boulder. 15 February 1987

Andy Grundberg. "Going Soft." in *SoHo News*, no. 31. London. 30 April-6 May 1980

Charles Hagen. "Francesca Woodman." in *The New York Times*, New York. 10 December 1993

Mary Ellen Haus. "Francesca Woodman". in *ARTnews*, New York. no. 1. April 1986

Faye Hirsch. "Old Geometry: The Photographs of Francesca Woodman." in *The Print Collector's Newsletter*, vol. XXV. no. 2. New York. May-June 1994

Lorraine Kenny. "Problem Sets: The Canonization of Francesca Woodman." in *Afterimage*, no. 4. New York. November 1986; see also "Letters." in *Afterimage*, no. 5. New York. December 1986

Bernard Lamarche-Vadel. "Francesca Woodman." in *Vis à vis*, no. 15. Paris. Spring 1994

Robert C. Morgan. "Francesca Woodman: Photographic Work." in *C.E.P.A. Quarterly*, vol. 2. no. 1. Buffalo. New York. Fall 1986

Stephen Perloff. "Four Snapshots." in *The Photo Review*, vol. 12. no. 4. Langhorne, PA. Fall 1989

Abigail Solomon-Godeau. "Our Bodies. our Icons." in *Vogue*, New York. February 1986

Margaret Sundell. "Vanishing Point: The Photography of Francesca Woodman." in *Inside the Visible*, MIT Press (ed.). Cambridge. Mass. and London. 1989

Roberta Valtorta. "Francesca Woodman." in *Progresso Fotografico*, Milan. no. 10. October 1976

Sylvia Wolf. "A Promise Cut Short." in *Art Week*, vol. 18. no. 16. Oakland. 25 April 1987

Publication

William A. Ewing. *The Body: Photographs of the Human Form*, Thames and Hudson Ltd.. London. 1994

Acknowledgements

Our greatest debt is to Betty and George Woodman without whom this book could not have been made. We are most grateful for their friendly and most precious help.

We would also like to thank the authors who contributed to this book: Philippe Sollers, David Levi Strauss, Elizabeth Janus and Sloan Rankin.

We are deeply indebted to people who knew Francesca Woodman and who have generously provided certain documents whose content has by now acquired capital importance: Besty Berne, Paolo Colombo, Ugo Ferranti, Giuseppe Gallo, Max Kozloff, Sabina Mirri, Edith Schloss, Anita Thatcher, Helen Miranda Wilson. Among them we would like to express our special thanks to Giuseppe Casetti and Piero Missigoi, former directors of the *Maldoror* bookshop.

Finally, the Fondation Cartier pour l'art contemporain expresses its thanks to all those who have contributed to this project through their advice, availability and enthusiasm: Eleanor Barefoot, Michael Branson, Giovanna Calvenzi, Rosella Caruso, Gianni Dessì, Janelle Lynch, Austin Thomas.

The institutions: Contrasto, Rome: Roberto Koch, Alessandra Mauro: Gary Edwards Gallery, Washington: Galerie Lelong, New York: Mary Sabbatino; La Nuova Pesa, Rome: Simona Marchini and Ombretta Orlandini: Metropolitan Museum, New York: Maria Morris Hambourg; RISD, Honors Program, Rome: Silvia Esposito; Whitney Museum of American Art, New York: Adam Weinberg.

This catalogue is published at the occasion of the exhibition *Francesca Woodman* presented at the Fondation Cartier pour l'art contemporain in Paris, from April 11 to May 31, 1998.

Curator: Hervé Chandès

Exhibition Coodinator: François Quintin assisted by Nathalie Rosticher

Catalogue: Dorothée Charles assisted by Caroline Edde, Anne Giraud, Gaëlle Lassée

---

Curator of the Fondation Cartier pour l'art contemporain
Hervé Chandès

Secretary General
Nicolas Bos

Assistants to the Curator
Véronique Baton, Hélène Kelmachter, Serge Laurent, Grazia Quaroni, François Quintin

Assistant Curator
Anne Vogt-Bordure

Nomadic Nights
Serge Laurent assisted by Caroline Dahan

Publications
Dorothée Charles assisted by Gaëlle Lassée

Press Relations
Linda Chenit, trainee: Vanessa Vion

Logistics Executive
Corinne Bocquet, trainee: Virginie Bergeron

Personnel Management
Françoise Vagné

Bookshop, Group Bookings
Vania Merhar

Secretariat
Michèle Geoffroy, Ursula Thai

Reception
François Gandziri

General Supervisory Support
François Romani

Installation of Works
Tony Negro

The exhibition *Francesca Woodman* is organized by the Fondation Cartier pour l'art contemporain under the aegis of the Fondation de France, and by the Cartier Company.

Hervé Chandès (ed.) — Francesca Woodman

Editing: Alexis Schwarzenbach

Translation: Rana Dasgupta, London

Design: Larry Kazal, Paris

Scanning and Printing: Le Govic, Nantes

Binding: SIRC, Marigny-le-Châtel

The original French edition of this book was
published in France by Fondation Cartier pour l'art contemporain
and Actes Sud.
© 1998 Fondation Cartier pour l'art contemporain
© 1998 Actes Sud

© 1998 for this edition:
Fondation Cartier pour l'art contemporain, Paris, and
Scalo Zurich—Berlin—New York
phone +41 1 261 0910, fax +41 1 261 9262,
e-mail publishers@scalo.com

Distributed in North America by D.A.P., New York City:
in Europe, Africa and Asia by Thames and Hudson, London:
in Germany, Austria and Switzerland by Scalo.

First Scalo Edition 1998
ISBN 3-931141-96-9 Printed in France